Burying the Wren

For Michael
(1965–2009)

Deryn Rees-Jones
Burying the Wren

SEREN

Seren is the book imprint of
Poetry Wales Press Ltd.
57 Nolton Street, Bridgend, Wales, CF31 3AE

www.serenbooks.com
Facebook: facebook.com/SerenBooks
Twitter: @SerenBooks

The right of Deryn Rees-Jones to be identified as
the author of this work has been asserted in accordance
with the Copyright, Designs and Patents Act, 1988.

© Deryn Rees-Jones 2012

ISBN: 978-1-85411-576-8
e-pub 978-1-85411-598-0
Kindle 978-1-78172-024-0

A CIP record for this title is available from the British Library.

The publisher acknowledges the financial assistance of the Welsh Books
Council.

Cover art: 'The Wren's Egg' by kind permission of Alice Maher.

Printed in the US in Bembo by Edwards Brothers Molloy, Ann Arbor, Michigan

Contents

I

II

III

IV

In a dark time, the eye begins to see,
I meet my shadow in the deepening shade;
I hear my echo in the echoing wood —
A lord of nature weeping to a tree,
I live between the heron and the wren,
Beasts of the hill and serpents of the den.
                                    — Roethke

The wren, the wren, the king of all birds,
On St. Stephen's Day was caught in the furze;
Up with the kettle and down with the pan,
Pray give us a penny to bury the wren.
                        — Traditional Irish Wren song

I

Three Glances at a Field of Poppies

The first, a pointillist's dream:
blood drop, an ache, or a smudge
of dolour.

★

Zoom in, where an ant tips a blade
of grass and the steps of its brothers
are footfalls of sorrow.

★

Now where? To the dark, where a seed
might sing, imagining a life
pushed into form, pure colour.

Burying the Wren

I kissed you at the corner gate,
our breath warmed with whisky and ale

and thought of that small brown bird
the Wren Boys brought:

soft as the hairs behind your ears –
so cold – the wren on the pole in her little box,

the fluttering breast you longed to touch.

A Dream of Constellations

When the months that were left could be held in our hands
I wanted to speak, but I could not. The astrocytal cells
that formed and grew inside your brain
following heart lines, speech lines, bedding in,
bringing you visions, disrupting your speech,
brought us a night that was suddenly known,
but not as itself. And so, like a dream about to be spoken,
silence buried itself in me. In this new pitch,

the navigated darkness of our life,
this telling and untelling of the world,
Time sped and slowed. The constellations shifted,
bringing us messages in particles of dust and light.
Together we looked up to the sky
as Ursa Minor became the headless bear,
the twin sons of Castor and Pollux, unexcellent, unsweet,
buried themselves beneath the earth,

and Vela's sail unfurled, became ragged.
Sagittarius the archer, staggered, wounded,
ripped his arm on a jagged star, unnamed for this instant;
together we wept for Berenice
with her one breast, with her shorn-off hair.
And as Time was slinking, doing its business,
the fiery empyreal nature of things
became the thing on which we most depended.

It was a new world, our night sky,
and I'd like to think the story of what lived between us then
expanded in the moment of our looking:
charting new maps in the darkness, allowing us to trust
that we might live by the light of the stars and their
reseedings, those wild celestial fields, which
hovered in the dashes and the dots.

After You Died

The night would not give in to me –
or something inside me would not yield.
The great harness of love I was wearing
stiffened in my shoulders, was held like a bit
between my teeth.
                    Last night
I woke and the moon was there,
her old romance of self-reliance and inconstancy.
And though my children in their turn
woke up to frantic dreams, were held,

brought back to bed,
she was there, her face full with a fierce singing.

And the dark again became a place
of sleep, a wild thing cohabiting.

Dogwoman

after Paula Rego

No one can love this horror, no one can want it.
I'm crouched between my own thighs

with my dog heart and my dog soul. For now I'm a woman
brought up by dogs, bitch in the muck and the blood and the dirt.

For once, now, I've got no words, and look
I'm trampling my bed, I'm baying at the moon.

And no one can hear me, with my skirts pulled up,
head back as my eyes roll. Look. I'm swallowing sorrow.

No one can hear me in spite of the howls.

★

I am lying on my back, my legs outsplayed.
That would be my dog-look, now, I'm giving you,

my half-cock, something askance and going to hell,
take me/leave me, inbreath/outbreath. Trembling,

I'm all upturned. Heart-hit, flesh-bound,
saying *love love* in a ring of devotion.

Here's my dogbelly with its small pink teats.
I'm waiting for the pressure

of your well-shaped hand.

★

Now dog's the divine. Strange thought. Dancing on hind legs,
head to one side, and the face of her master. Dog sudden, well-met.

Dog sitting, dog listening, dog running with big joy
and ghost dogs on the fields now with her. Dog blur,

hellhound, dog shaking, hare-bound; dog in the wind, sky-bound.
(Once, attendant in my blue dress, I hadn't the words to call you back.)

Dog in the snow, dog in the sea. Dog glorious, glories herself.
Dog racing with gleam and thunder. Best friend. Neither

fish nor fowl. Just for this moment, hound bliss.

★

Now dog sleeps, dead to the world. Dog faithful. Dog tired.
Dog whose faint stink, dog-breath, under the dog star

is dog waiting, dog at heel. There's no one to love
this sleeping dog. Dogsuckle, dogwash. Dog with her master,

dog in a manger. Dog cradle. Dog holding.
Here now with her lover's body. Upstairs. Downstairs. Dog now

with her dogheart split. Rough courage. Dog mutter.
Dog pause. Moans, stirs.

Words now are never enough.

★

Dog tricks and the memory of dogs, dogs dreaming
and not in colour. Dog fetching, dog on a leash,

dog watching, dog weeps. Dog fond, dog mother.
Dog sniff. Dog holler. God of dogs, dog love.

Dog sent to bed in deep disgrace. Dog shock, piss, squalor.
And joy, dearest, tail wag. Dog rhythm, dog riff,

dog's domain and death's dominion.
The body's frame's not enough for itself,

these pale fires of horror.

★

Flea-bitten, dog-eared. At the centre there's a hole, or rather rent,
a tent-flap in the wind. Dog blood. Dog mess. Dog foaming

at the gates of hell. And, where words will neither cure nor reason
dog's here, fur-matted, nose wet. Lap dog, dog of the dead,

wide-mawed, tongue lolling. Dog in the dark destroying the world.
Dog killer, dog doper, dolling out medicine, taking her pills.

And who in the world could not love a dog? Dog rhyme. Dog bold.
Guantánamo dog in her orange jumpsuit.

Girl on the mountainside, dog girl at her bones.

★

Now I've a look of something else, leg drawn to my shoulder.
Dog woman whose dog limbs quiver; dogwoman

and my teeth are bared. A plastic collar might do the trick
to stop me gnawing at flesh and fur. Dog alert and

no one to touch her. Dog gesture, rat-catcher.
Dog least likely. Dog outstretched. Dog-snout,

snarling, hollering. The flowering armpit of a gramophone.
So here we are, in the veiny dark. Here's

the moment of pain when the music holds.

★

Had I once known my dog self – whelp, cur – the
dog skull, dog rose, hair of the dog from shoulder to paw,

good dog/bad dog from which I came, wouldn't I now
in this stiff chair ask you again, letting things slip,

my head resting on your furry pelt, head lifted
to the pink of your maw? And how would I know,

and would you be glad, of this dog bright
pricking her ears? Dog in the mud. Dog in the dust.

Wouldn't I ask you not to go?

★

Dog gentle in the good night. Dog lost, hunkers here.
Dogwoman, dogsoul. Breath escaping

the bone cage, faster. Dog refusing to leave her master.
Dog gentle, dog love, dog left in the wild machine

of dog grizzle, dog slobber, holding you now
it is over and over. Licking and weeping,

a body cools. Woman loving. Dog gone. I am
speaking/not speaking an unspeakable prayer.

And now I am kneeling, dog alone.

★

Alert in the darkness, head to one side, dog's very still.
And then I see her at her own side, waiting.

Particle, matter, dog in the moonlight.
Trees cast their shadows. The day hunkers down.

From the black leaves of night she creeps, very slowly. Quietly,
with her dog eyes closed. Out of blood, out of debris,

snuffling, singing, settling skirts and shaping
the emptiness, dog howling, dog waking.

Doggedly dogging, dog being born.

★

This slow love as snow falls becomes elsewhere
the fierce heat at the core of ourselves. Dogs jumping up,

tangled in wildflowers. Dogs in a waterfall, dogs at the beach.
Dogs reading books under African starlight. Dog with her nose now

pressed to the window. Dog in the cold. Dog in the dark.
Dogs crying and frisking the limitless reaches.

Dogs on their cliff edge, not looking down. And
love in the things that can't be unbroken. Love in the skies

where I cannot yet follow. Love, in these strange times, passage of souls.

II

Trilobite

Remember, as a child, how someone would shout *Catch!*
and too old to refuse, and too young not to,
the body's coordinates not quite set

this object, moving in an arc towards you
somehow created you, trembling, outstretched?
That's how it came to me, this trilobite,

a present from the underworld, a stern familiar
hopelessly far-fetched. What it wanted from me
I never knew, its hard parts being its only parts,

the three parts of its crossways nature
cephalos, thorax, pigidium
as later, now, I've learned to call them,

carrying a memory of itself like water
as my fingers moved on its captive body,
the feathery stone of its cool guitar.

It reminded me of a woodlouse, too,
the honesty of small, friendly things.
But the metallic gleam of its smoothed edges

were taut and innocent as an unfired gun.
So it bedded in, leaving behind a gleaming trail
as a biro bleeding in a pocket might,

a puff of ink from a hounded squid.
And my skin shimmered
with its silvery threads, and my breath quickened

as it wrote my body, left a garden of knowing in damp tattoos.
The further I threw it, the closer it came.
Sometimes, alone, I'd ask it questions

stroke it like a secret pet.
How deep is the ocean? What's the blueness of blue?
How is the earth as you lie inside it?

It would reply in a voice both
high-pitched and enduring, or
whisper like a ghost till only silence remained.

And left me only when I'd learned to love it,

small as a bullethole,
in the place where it pressed itself,
its fossil colours close to my heart.

Last night, unable to sleep,
it nudged its way back into my life,
pulling me from the fragrant pillow

to perch once again on my naked shoulders,
to drop like a coin in my offered hand.
Beside me, my husband slept.

And the fact of its presence, its subtle truth,
was something to touch,
like the wounds of Christ;

its transformation as I went to kiss it,
a wafer on the pushed-out tongue.

Truffles

The Umbrian black truffle,
a delicacy in these mulish towns,

was born, or so the Romans had it,
when lightning struck the earth,

secreting a nugget of heavenly fire
in oak or hazel woods

whose altitude and climate,
calcerous soils, combine to breed

the truffle's strength,
its heady auras known

by sweating housewives, perfumed chefs
to make electric any humdrum dish:

a fungus potent, so we read,
as the pheromones

of two wild boars – known also
for their sense of smell –

whose butchered testicles emit
a scent more dangerous to some

than Japanese beetles, gypsy moths,
or Circe with her plaited hair

who tosses acorns, feckless men,
into the hot Aeaean mud.

More pungent, then, than mountain goats
whose cheese we daub on rounds of bread,

the amoretti which we dip in wine, or,
hemmed with rosemary and mint,

the sunflower fields where,
like the truffle hunters, too, this burning

afternoon, we root out treasure for ourselves
until we've harvested each spore

from armpit, neck, from groin,
enthralled by subterranean gods

who now make dogs of us, or swine,
till we lie senseless in the dirt,

hearts splitting in the heat.

A Chinese Lacquer Egg

Something is beginning. We feel it in the raw edges
of our dreams, our bodies hostage to light, to weather.
It is filling us with the weight of summer
which floats like helium through our wintered bones.
We wonder at it all, surprised by warmth, a sudden downpour,
the ruffled line of birdsong, a forgotten bulb
forcing its way through sodden earth towards the sun.
Or this Chinese lacquer egg, which appeared one morning
in my outstretched palm. Beyond the sound
of aeroplane or train, as we drift asleep, hands cupped
to the pillow, it shares its oval mysteries. Listen!
Between breath and silence it is showing itself.
In these shortened nights it is not unlike rapture,
an unworded prayer its indelible hum.

Shaved Fennel with Blood Oranges, Pomegranate, Pecorino

i.m. Thom Gunn

It's one of those moments, the radio on,
light creeping through the kitchen
on a early summer's evening
and then the sudden piercing, a voice announcing
that you're dead. It mingles, now,
with the smell of fennel,
blood oranges, and ewe's milk cheese,
green seeds and lemons, pomegranates,
a dish served up, that night, a funeral plate for one.
It is food to take the winter out of all of us,
calling us as even now,
with its muscular flexing in foetal turns
I call my own child on.

Couvade

Like that tribe of South Americans
who raise a sympathetic magic
from a woman's growing foetus
piercing themselves in unspeakable places
and hanging under torture in the rafters,
bird's eye witnesses in agony
at the moment of their baby's birth

you've taken this pregnancy to heart
as daily you grow listless, unsteady
in the mornings, muttering
in your afternoon sleep,
craving fruits or nursery foods,
bland textures, carbohydrates,

a sweet tooth running amok,
limbs thickening, waist rounding out;
your auburn hair like the mane of a horse
but as Strabo observed, looking better
than most, with darkening areolae,
high-flushed cheeks, the smile of Valentinus.

Daughter II

Blake's angel, what makes you?
Blood, bone, mineral? The black space
that creates the universe, would

if it could, suck everything in?
Sometimes
I hardly dare look, the night

losing its face to the senses
as you, with those owlish eyes
little ribs, not long since

shocked into light
and an appetite
and your damp hair like feathers

nuzzle in beside me,
no one to answer,
or to answer to. Only

an unlearned joy when you wake
which is ours: your breath on my skin
enough to stop a heart,

to darn the threadbare morning.

Aderyn Yr Eira

Starling

Against the green-black of the sleek night sky
the burning love of a mother and a daughter:
stars made into snow, and vice versa.

Slugs

Each night the slugs have found a way of getting in.
They slip through cracks, inhabiting corners,
edging up table-legs, walls, or chairs.
With their slug etiquette, slug gestures,
are they silently dreaming of lettuces, hostas?
Do they elegise greenhouses, commune with their dead?
Or fantasize brethren on distant planets?
What mistakes do they make, and how will they tell us?
Do we ask their forgiveness? Do they imagine us saved?
Of their psychobiographies will I ever be sure?

Occipital horns conduct in the darkness.
They know nothing of envy, nothing of blame.
In the gastropod inchings of their midnight seances,
the slow rehearsals of molluscular dance,
they're themselves absolutely, beyond imitation.
And their silvery cast offs Isadora's
just at the moment in the silvery moonlight
when she sheds her scarves to a million stars.

Hallucigenia

(i)

The room where I imagine you, my eyes unclosed
to its supposéd windows, floors, eventually misleads me
so that even now we're years ago with different lives
and dumb voyeurs to this: two bodies
catching at each other, light.
Such faithlessness for us becomes a kind of death.
What helps is this: that pleasure's
something made from love as well.
Denying it, taking it up, would hurl us out of time
away from our more equal loves
and everything outside that can't be fitted
into just one life/two lives.
And so a look that stirs can make belief itself more right,
more real, in fact, more dear, and no impediment.

(ii)

Ok. But as we're in that room I've brought you to,
our stanza out of time, out of our depth, let's say
on the muddy floor of the Burgess Shale
where velvet worms and arthropods
whose spiky backs and stumpy legs,
whose compound eyes imprint
themselves, *hallucigenia*, in rock,
let words, which like the fossils
make a house for us in lexical delight,
open the world to reimagine us,
to catch the imprint of our softened parts
which as my mouth now, line by line,
is emptied into yours, becomes a different silence
from the first, in commas, dashes and full stops.

My Grandfather's Tattoo

On sunny days, his shirtsleeves rolled,
he'd cover with a sticking plaster –
like the wound of Welsh he wouldn't give his children –
the blue-green inks of anchorage, the shame.

Daughter III

It's peacock, she says, and holds up the stained-glass page to the light;
or, pomegranate, she decides, returning to colour
the jewels of its hundred eyes.

L

Some mysteries are never solved: the tongue of flame,
the rolled back stone, the body's weight
when it walks on water; or even the tale
of the Capuchin priest who for fifty years
wore the wounds of Christ, was drenched in the odour
of holy blood, his body healed at his last confession:
Maria! he whispered, bowing his head,
dying the death of a little bird
as he stood before the gates of heaven.

Which takes me back to that night in San Andreas
and the barbell I found, caught like a thorn
between mattress and sheet. Or was it a dream,
the blue of her skin between ligament and bone,
her arm bent like the letter L, as she washed your feet
with her hennaed hair? The blemish on your palm
between headline and heartline, a faultline,
like her name, or the scent she wore,
the line of a song you won't remember.

III

from *The Songs of Elisabeth So*

I notice, now, that you've lost weight,
your hair is cropped, your body somehow smaller;
and square and unfamiliar the lines of your dark suit

that show your gait has found a new lopsidedness,
the way our year-old son in shoes
adjusts his body to – and us the heart –

new freight;
and finds me, as I wait here, only sad.

And I don't want, I find, those flowers
that used to spring up with your look,
then fade and darken at your passing.

The corridors are singing with your hurt.
Take songs away, take flowers away, take too
the gentle artfulness of your restraint.

★

You call me Elisabeth, which I like,
Elisabeth *So*, Elisabeth *Please*.
And you undress me in a dream.
And so you tease...

Forgive me these,
as words, my love,
unhook, undo.
And do not move

until I'm there spelled out with you.
The bed is awake with us at last.
Your name is one
I will not speak.
Don't ask, don't ask me to.

★

Whose mouth is this in the roomy darkness,
whose hand is this that flies with mine,
who sails with me in the room in the darkness,
whose body slips with mine through time.

Whose voice is this that calls me, calls me,
who runs beside me like the wind,
who holds me as the ocean pulls me,
who holds me, word to word, a rhyme.

Tell me, what shall we do with this hour of abundance?
What shall we do with this hour of wonder?
What is the best way to sing our praise?

I ask and ask but you will not answer.

My mouth is yours – if only you'd answer,
to prove the darkness and the silence wrong.

★

We're out of season, out of luck,
the day pot-boiled to its unlovingness.
So go.

Like a wronged god, or a ghost,
I never wanted you.
For we are not a rhyming pair,

we are not in the one breath,
not the morning's sudden clear air.
We are not the surge

and swell, the ocean's rhythm.
We are
not even a plywood plane thrown up into the sky;

ours is not this kind of gladness.
We're so unlovely and so small.
Know that as we lie together here.

★

It was the only blessing that I asked you for,
of leaving me unnoticed –
like the earth might tree seeds or a rouged leaf
in its fall.

Instead, you give me nothing,
catch me inside your coat
to see if you can catch my breath,

steal me, my soul,

which slipping through me, in an instant, rises up
and hovers near the smell of you.

The thumping of your chest to which I'm otherwise immune
has left me on the wind's breath, now.
It was the blessing that I asked you for.

Instead you leave me trembling here, a feather.

★

The gentle artfulness of your restraint is what, of course, I love;
the gentleness that as I sit beside you
I can't prove.

Just like the look you give which, though I see,
I must refuse to catch and hold, as I imagine you'd
hold me.

But my hands, beside yours in the sunlight, can't refrain
from singing as I hold them in my lap;
and then a thousand birds begin to rise.

They sing and fly in the singing light
and the room is suddenly full of their music.
And I do not care that they will not listen.

And I do not care that they will not stop.

IV

Shrub & Willow

Shrub's heart was a box, a certainty.
While Willow played, let out her hair to the rheumy breeze
Shrub was inviolable, a taut high wire.

Willow on the banks of the still river, raised her head to
                                        check the sadness.
How like that mermaid with human feet
was her walking through silence, her dancing on glass.

Shrub was a sentry on the steps of the house.
Shrub was anger, Shrub was despair.
Perhaps Willow was love, an hysterical air.

Yet blood ran between them. And how will it be, my unlikely pair,
O my Willow, my Shrub,
in the forest's night when I find you there?

The Fetch

When she came, her eyes shielded against the light,
it was as if we'd always known she would:
her dark hair and her eyes like apple pips.
From whose head had she sprung?

She was calling me in the silence of puddles,
cloudfall, a rise of starlings to the darkening nights,
                              sap sticky in the dew.
Twice she came and then again,
her heart exposed, espaliered across her ribs,

her face pressed to the window.

I watched her that last time as she walked across the room.

She carried in the velvet pockets of her coat
bittercress, dogviolets,
and, like the memory of the shape of a book,
        a solitary duck egg,
blown,
        its melancholy blue.

The Box

I'd asked for calico to line the box
and though you'd passed

so far from self, and I
still wandered, something was at rest.

On the funeral day, I came again:
your lips were cold, your eyelid stitched.

And later it was Pam, not I,

who laid the turf from Mayo at your feet,
the lilacs on your chest.

A Scattering

I am standing by the waters where we've let you rest:
candles, ashes, seven roses set like seven boats

into the lough. The rain has stopped
and our daughter dances.

Where is our son?
Way up high on his great-uncle's shoulders.

A swan's wing, limp, instead of my arm,
I'm a bride to silence, these smaller spaces,

the mist like breath on the landscape's glass.

Chinese Lanterns

Bright crepe on summer nights, a carnival
of melancholy heat, a row of pumpkin-headed smiles.
Their skeletons are metaphors to wear against the dark
who wear their loss barefoot
like sad fluorescent dancers.

Peony

Such intimacy when I press into the darkness of its heart.
As if it were a friend of mine
– like love – like death –
I speak to it of this and that, I furnish it with whispers.

Moon River

They're not the words I'm thinking of,
but the tune comes back the same.
And all the lives we've never wanted.
Your face in the huckleberry river.
Holly Golightly running through the New York rain.

Kinks

Hitting a hairpin bend in fourth, I'd be forgiven
for calling you everything under the sun, our rock and roll
on the empty road, as life, now, flashes before me,
moving me from fear to love.

And would I be forgiven, too, in the darkening room,
for seeing last night a likeness
to that honey-bear the Kinkajou?

Who, sipping nectar from a balsa-blossom bud
had your face, and so took my breath,
dusted with light as it was, and pollen.

Ellipsis

And there I found myself, more truly and more strange.
                       – Wallace Stevens

★

I had started to think of the skin ego,
of *Women, Fire and Dangerous Things,*
the lost books, fluttering, opening their wings like veins...

★

Perhaps it was a false start, the veined blue
remembering of a breast, the scent of milk
in that photograph, the coil of your double crown as you fed.

★

But words like bandages were slowly unravelling...
and somewhere I was becoming the dreamwork of my life,
every room in the house now blunted

to an irrational fear of knives, maybe,
the glittering wage of the umbilicus,
the navel of the dream.

★

And the blue heartstopping pulse at the wrist
was insistent as a rhyme
unstitching itself...

the red stain of the past
on my improbably stretched-out hands.

Stillborn

These days, I lie awake,
picking from beneath my skin –
a reassembling in the dark –
two gleaming eyes, a beating heart,
pink on the cheeks like a daisy's edge, my brother:
fragments of tooth and bone.

Letter From Marrakesh

for Kate

The swifts are flying across the medina....
A sudden storm has blown pink sand across the souk
and Alex wonders do you want an ostrich egg?

A wild dog ate, alas! the lonely tortoise in the garden.
An old umbrella doubles as a parasol.
Our children's texts like bird prints in the snow....

In the Djemaa El Fna you wander through the crowds:
the fire-eaters and storytellers, tooth-pullers, acrobats....
These days are all that is ahead of us.

Come soon, you write, *come soon*....

Each night, a great white owl
like the moon, missing its step in the sky,
swoops down to drink the silver swimming pool.

Meteor

And this is how everything vanishes,
how everything that vanishes begins,
the hinged moment looking forwards and back.
Like that night when we sat with the back door open,
the summer distilled to the scent of jasmine,
the scrape of cutlery, the chink of glass.
A robin stirred in the dusty hedgerow.
Clothes held our bodies as a mouth might a kiss.
Then the meteor brought us to our feet:
a stripped atom, trapping electrons
to excite the darkness with its violet light.
I remember how it disturbed the heavens,
burned against the air to leave no trace.

Persephone

Some days it is simple,
the way outside turns inner,

the fall towards light,
the pull of the weather.

This is love's work –
the way I've learnt again to slip inside my dreams:

to hold my face up to the rain,
move from one world to another.

Tom-Tom

A last gift from my father.

And I think of him now as I slip through gears:
the satellites are calling, the coordinates are set.

Where we are going and how we are getting there
is all we need to know...and this is what he most remembered:

my propensity for getting lost.

Is it his voice trailing from the heavens?

Like one of Ovid's beasts transformed,
the tom-tom like a brave's heart beat.

Burying The Wren

(Coda)

So these are the dog days
when the sea boils, and the wine turns sour;

when the sky thunders, and the house cries out:
Dearest, you promised you'd be near.

One day, you'd just fetched up.
Love me, I said. Who else was there

to step into my thorny heart,
who knew enough in their half-life,

of soul-mess, blather, to take my hand
in the dark wood

and walk with me away?
Now this might be my hardest weather.

You call to me and call again.
O skittish I am all astray.

★

If I look up now when the sky burns black
perhaps I can remember this:

your way of leaving us and our long night,
love-blessing, liturgy,

the prayer of the unholy,
and getting you −

death rattle, heart-stop −
to where the struggle ends,

sending you in the longboat of your body
where worlds and words collide, was not

the end of love. Yet love
you've been with me enough,

so I must let you be, remove myself from the
cool earth, where weeds will blossom, rivers run,

your pyre of turf that burns
along a drift of speedwell and bogthistle,

primrose, pimpernel and vetch,
where rain will learn to fall once more

and lightning bring its electricity
to animate the uncaged heart.

Here, where a wren sings, flirty in the alder,
in the long hot days of May,

when you are three years gone.

Acknowledgements and Notes

Acknowledgements are due to the editors of the following publications where versions of these poems first appeared: *American Poet, The Amsterdam Review, Dark Matter: Poems of Space, The Manhattan Review, New Writing* 10, *New Welsh Review, Planet, Poetry London, Poetry Review, Poetry Wales, The Reader, Wild Reckoning: Poems provoked by Rachel Carson's Silent Spring, Best Poems of 2011.* Some of these poems have also appeared in the chapbook *Falls & Finds* (Shoestring, 2008). 'The Wren's Egg' was part of a collaboration with Alice Maher for the AHRC *Poetry Beyond Text* project. 'Three Glances at a Field of Poppies' was commissioned by the National Wildflower Centre as a response to 'The New Urban Green' Exhibition.

Burying the Wren
The parading of a wren in a holly branch or box by the Wren Boys in Ireland on St. Stephen's Day is a custom that still exists. Traditionally the Wren Boys, dressed in masks, would move from house to house, asking for money to bury the wren. The ritual killing of the wren in midwinter also appears as a tradition in parts of Wales, the Isle of Man and Southern France. The wren is noted for its loud and complex song, sometimes as part of a duet, even in the wintertime.

Aderyn yr Eira
Welsh for starling, literally, bird of the snow.

Hallucigenia
An extinct genus of animal, named for its dream-like, hallucinogenic quality.

Also by Deryn Rees-Jones

Poems

The Memory Tray
Signs Round a Dead Body
Quiver
Falls and Finds

Criticism

Carol Ann Duffy
Consorting with Angels: Modern Women Poets

As editor

Contemporary Women's Poetry: Reading/Writing/Practice
(with Alison Mark)
Modern Women Poets
Writing Liverpool: Essays and Interviews (with Michael Murphy)
Michael Murphy, Collected Poems
Marie Stopes, Love's Creation